THE APPLE OF HIS EYE

SEEING YOURSELF THROUGH GOD'S EYES

ASHER INTRATER

Original manuscript published by Destiny Image, Shippensburg, PA, 1990.
ISBN 1-56043-414-7.

This edition published by Revive Israel Media, 206 East 4th Street, Frederick, MD 21701. www.reviveisrael.org

Cover design and interior layout by www.PearCreative.ca

ISBN 978-0-9891926-0-6

For Worldwide Distribution

Printed in the USA

CONTENTS

THE HUMAN POTENTIAL

Go into any bookstore today or look at any magazine rack, and you will find such themes running through the titles as: realizing your potential, the secret of success, the winning formula, the power of positive thinking, developing your self-image, and so on.

The world knows that there is some great untapped power within a human being, but they do not know what it is, where it comes from, or how to get it out.

King Solomon said that God had placed "eternity" in the hearts of men (Ecclesiastes 3:11), but that they could not understand it. For lack of better understanding, scientists have sometimes referred to this deep inner capacity as the subconscious mind. In fact, it is not the mind at all but the spirit of the man that contains the deep inner resources.

God is a spirit being and man is created in His image. Man is aware that there is something of great importance within his inner being. Man is yearning to see the realization of that infinite potential from within. The answer is not to be found in human self-actualization techniques. The answer lies rather in discovering who we are in relationship with an infinite and personal God in whose image we are created.

Years ago, in pondering the purpose and potential of man, King David asked a question similar to what many are asking today.

Psalm 8:4-5

What is man that You are mindful of him, and the son of man that You visit him? For You have made him a little lower than the angels, and You have crowned him with glory and honor.

This book is designed to answer that question and to help you be all that you can be in God.

CHAPTER 1
HOW VALUABLE YOU ARE

The first step in our relationship with God is to understand that He loves us and that we are very special in His sight. We are the object of His affection as is any child in the eyes of his father.

> **Matthew 6:25**
> **Therefore, I say to you, do not worry about your life—what you will eat or what you will drink, nor about your body, what you will put on. Is not life more than food, and the body more than clothing?**

Yeshua (Jesus) makes a clear distinction between your body and you. You as a person are worth a certain value to God, and the body that you are clothed with has a separate value. You and your body are not the same. You are clothed with a body. You dwell in a body. You move about in a body as in a vehicle, but you are not your body. You are a spiritual being made in the image of God.

I live inside a body much the way I dwell in a house. I live inside a house and my house reflects my personality. If you were to come into a house and find it all filthy and in disrepair, you would know that it could not be my house if you knew me personally. In a similar way, the real you is the living personality within. Your life, activities, clothing and so on will reflect the personality of the invisible man within. The importance of you as a person is much greater than your mere physical attributes.

Matthew 6:26
Look at the birds of the air, for they neither sow, nor reap, nor gather into barns. Yet your heavenly Father feeds them. Are you not of much more value than they?

Yeshua asks us to consider this key question: "Are you not of much more value than they?" Every single one of us must ask ourselves whether our own estimation of our self worth is in line with God's estimation of us. Are we not of more value than the birds of the air?

In the gospel of Luke, Yeshua is quoted making the same point:

Luke 12:6-7
Are not five sparrows sold for two copper coins? And not one of them is forgotten before God. But the very hairs on your head are all numbered.

In other words, God knows about even the smallest details of your life, and He is concerned about all of them.

Luke 12:7
Do not fear, therefore. You are of more value than many sparrows.

Once again we find this key phrase: "You are of great value." It takes a supernatural revelation of grace to know that you are important to God. Can you grasp that? You are not of little value, nor are you worthless. You are of great value. You are special, and God loves you.

WHAT DOES GOD CARE ABOUT?

The apostle Paul states the same thing in his first letter to the Corinthians:

> ### I Corinthians 9:8-10
> **Do I say these things as a mere man? Or does not the Law say the same thing also? For it is written in the Law of Moses, "You shall not muzzle an ox while it treads out the grain." Is it about oxen that God is concerned? Or does He say this altogether for our sakes? For our sakes, no doubt, this is written.**

Paul is explaining that money given into the ministry may be used to pay for the financial needs of the ministers. He makes this explanation by quoting Deuteronomy 25:4 where the Law is speaking of an agricultural principle not to withhold an animal from eating out of the very grain it is helping to harvest. Out of simple natural kindness, you would allow the ox to eat some of the grain that it is treading out.

Paul draws out this principle to make a point. He applies it by comparison to the money given to the ministry for the pastor's salary. Paul goes on from there to yet another comparison of much greater importance. He asks the question, "Is God primarily concerned with oxen?" Is the multitude of various animal species and plant life the primary concern of God? What is highest on God's priority list? Is it sparrows? Oxen? Houses? Buildings? Clothing? Or does God primarily care about people?

Obviously, it is people that God cares about. God cares about you. You are special to Him.

INTERPRETING SCRIPTURE

In this verse Paul is giving a very profound insight concerning Bible interpretation. When you read Scriptures, you are not to think primarily of philosophical issues or ritual laws or codes of conduct. Every verse of Scripture is about you, about people.

I Corinthians 9:10
Or does He say this [in Scripture] altogether for our sakes? For our sakes, no doubt, this is written.

What is written in Scripture is for our sakes. Scripture is not the sum total of all of God's knowledge, but rather those things that God wanted written down for our sakes. They are His particular thoughts that have to do with instructing and benefiting us. The underlying meaning of each verse has something to do with a personal connection between us and God. If the verse were not for that purpose, it would not be written in Scripture. There is no Scriptural revelation given for mere intellectual curiosity or theorizing. Scripture is given "altogether" for our sakes. For our benefit, "no doubt," it was written down as Scripture. Paul makes the same point at the end of his second letter to the Corinthians.

II Corinthians 12:19
...we speak before God in Messiah. But we do all things, beloved, for your edification.

II Corinthians 13:10
Therefore I write these things . . . according to the authority which the Lord has given me for edification.

All that which is spoken by the prophets, which is written in Scripture, and which is done by the ministry is for the purpose of edifying human beings. Edifying means to build up. God's motivation is to love us, to help us, to rescue us and make us whole, to get us out of the mess we have gotten ourselves into. He desires to restore us to the way He originally meant us to be. Any religious activity or theology which is not moving toward that goal is counter-productive.

The apostle John stated that everything he wrote was for the purpose of strengthening the faith of those who read it. He wrote it so that they could receive the life force of God and prosper in Him (John 19:35; 20:31; I John 1:4; 5:13; III John 2; Revelation 1:3; 22:6,14). The commandments of the Law of Moses were given so that those who obey them can be blessed in doing so (Deuteronomy 28:1ff). The proverbs of Solomon were recorded to show that Wisdom is calling out to instruct people out of their foolish and self-destructive ways (Proverbs 1:2,20; 4:1,5; 7:1; 8:1-5). What Yeshua did in His ministry was not to show off God's omnipotence. He did not come to emphasize how puny we are, but to destroy the power of the devil and to forgive us of our sins (John 10:10; Luke 24:47; Hebrews 2:14).

A THEOLOGY OF LOVE

All of the commandments of the Bible can be summed up by saying that we are to love God and love one another (Mark 12:30-31). Every verse of Scripture is for you. It is to express God's love to you. It is about the fact that you are special to God. You are the apple of His eye. You are the object of His affection. It is not oxen or anything else that God is concerned about. It is altogether for you. Why is Scripture written? – For you.

God's motivation is to benefit you and to speak something into your life that will change you and edify you. You are on the top of God's priority list. You are what God is concerned about. God's primary motive is His love for you. The primary theme of Scriptures is what God is doing to rescue you and restore your life. We interpret Scriptures by asking how it affects us personally and how it causes God's life and purity to come into us.

Arguments over theology usually do not have to do with how to bring God's life into people. To every philosophical disagreement we can say, "God is not concerned with oxen."

If we take the perspective of trying to edify those who hear us, we will be drawn into unity. For example, in deliverance from demonic spirits, the issue is not when, whether or where a person can have a demon, but how to get the person free from the influence of the devil. When we concentrate on how to benefit people, we will enter into the unity of faith.

God cares about you. He does not care about church pews other than to give people a place to sit. He does not care about economic theory other than how it affects your receiving of His provisions. He does not care about denominational organizations other than the well-being of the people in them.

RELIGIOUS CONDEMNATION

Religious tradition, as opposed to scriptural truth, often portrays human beings as worthless in the sight of God. "You are no good. You are of no value. You are dirty," says the voice of religious condemnation. The devil is called a liar and a deceiver, but he is also called an accuser and a condemner. The primary purpose of deception is to make you sin. The moment you sin, Satan changes his role from tempter into prosecuting attorney. First, he tempts you to sin and then he condemns you to death. God's desire is to raise us up (I Peter 5:6), and the devil's desire is to put us down. God humbles us first in order to raise us up afterward.

There is a difference between the conviction of sins and condemnation. The Holy Spirit brings conviction of sin so that God's goodness can lead us to repentance, and we can stop sinning.

Religious doctrine that condemns you is misrepresenting God. There is no condemnation in Messiah Yeshua (Romans 8:1). There is no condemnation that comes from God as long as we obey and trust Him. The way we receive condemnation is to leave the influence of God's grace. Many people do reject God and thereby receive condemnation. However, that condemnation is caused by rebelling against God and not by His intention against us. He is grace; He is love; He is forgiveness; He is also holiness.

If you walk out of the light, you are in darkness. In a certain sense, the light demonstrates the fact that you are in darkness because of the contrast. But it is not the fault of the light that you left its presence. God is light. There is no darkness in Him. All light is in Him. If you leave God's presence, you have to be in darkness. There is no light other than that which is in God.

Religious condemnation is the opposite of divine grace. The devil is a liar. The devil is the condemner; the damner. Religious condemnation is not of God. That is incorrect doctrine. Religion is the ministry of condemnation. Redemption is the ministry of God's grace.

> ### John 3:17-19
> **For God did not send His Son into the world to condemn the world, but that the world through Him might be saved. He who believes in Him is not condemned; but he who does not believe is condemned already... And this is the condemnation, that the light has come into the world, and men loved darkness rather than light, because their deeds were evil.**

The revelation of Scripture points out the fact that men have defiled themselves and turned away from God. Men have sinned and have placed themselves under condemnation. The world is in a very bad condition. It does not take too much wisdom to realize that. It does require, however, a supernatural revelation to know how to get us out of the mess we are in.

Scripture reveals the fact that all men are under condemnation, but it does not leave them there. The purpose of scriptural revelation is to get men out of that condemnation, not to lock them into it. Preaching convicts us of sin and then frees us from condemnation. A person has to stop sinning in order to come to a place where he will be free from condemnation.

SELF-RIGHTEOUSNESS IS FILTHY

The fact that all men are under condemnation is absolutely true. Without the intervening grace of God through Yeshua, every person is heading straight toward an everlasting torment. There is no way for man to get himself out of this disastrous situation.

The very nature of the human race has been so poisoned by Satan that no one can stand before God without guilt. Our sins have separated us from God. It is not a question of doing some good deeds but of getting our entire personality and inner being radically transformed. You cannot see the solution to a problem unless you see what the nature of that problem is.

You cannot receive the revelation of how to become the righteousness of God unless you recognize first that you have been completely unrighteous. What may seem right and moral to many people is still utterly despicable in relation to a perfectly pure and righteous God. Do not be deceived. Unless a person receives the grace of God through Yeshua's death and resurrection, he is damned for eternity.

Attempts by people to justify themselves in the sight of God are actually repulsive. It is as if someone has betrayed you personally and then comes to you to tell you how wonderful he is because he gave some money to charity. The more he tries to prove to you how deserving he is of your respect, the more you feel like getting him out of your presence.

Trying to prove yourself right does not work. The only valid thing to do is ask for forgiveness. God says that our attempts to prove our own self-righteousness are like a filthy menstrual rag in His sight (Isaiah 64:6). Self-righteousness is humanism. Humanistic self-righteousness is just as bad as religious condemnation.

How does God see us? Through Yeshua, He sees us as beloved, long lost children who have returned home. Without Yeshua, we are enemies who have betrayed God in the most detestable way.

MERCY BRINGS REPENTANCE

The Bible contains many passages of strong rebuke and judgment. These passages must be seen in the greater context of God's redeeming love. For example, even at the time of the plagues of the Exodus, God's primary purpose was not to destroy the Egyptians, but to rescue His covenant people Israel. In the previous generation, God blessed the Egyptians abundantly. His ultimate desire is to bring the Egyptians into harmony with Israel and to prosper them together (Isaiah 19:24-25).

Sometimes a parent has to bring a strong word of correction. This chastisement is not done to make the child feel bad or to put him down, but in the firm loving hope of seeing the child turn for the better. Some people are motivated to godliness by severe warnings; others by positive promises. The word "gospel" means good news. Yet that good news has a terrifying alternative if we do not receive it. We give love and truth to people in order to touch their consciences and move them toward what is right. Repentance is a positive solution to a horrible situation.

> ### Romans 2:4
> **Do you despise the riches of His goodness, forbearance, and longsuffering, not knowing that the goodness of God leads you to repentance?**

This attitude is motivation by grace. Everyone has his own free will. We are not to coerce people by psychological pressure or manipulation. Using the laws of righteousness in Scripture to condemn others is one of the earmarks of hypocrisy. Yeshua chased away the hypocrites who were trying to condemn the woman who had been caught in adultery. Obviously she was wrong. God does not condone sin. Even then, the best way to move her to repentance was to show her grace. That grace was coupled with a stern admonition not to sin again.

John 8:11
Yeshua said to her, "Neither do I condemn you; go and sin no more."

Even in this case, to minister condemnation to her was wrong. Some leaders try to motivate their people by guilt manipulation. This is wrong and you should not receive it.

MERCY TRIUMPHS OVER JUDGMENT

How do we reconcile God's mercy with His judgment? God's mercy is greater than His judgment. However, mercy only goes into effect when we realize that we are deserving of judgment.

James 2:13
Judgment is without mercy to the one who has shown no mercy. Mercy triumphs over judgment.

Judgment can only be seen in the light of God's mercy. Judgment results when a human being has rejected God's mercy in his life. Mercy is the greater principle. Mercy triumphs over judgment whenever the two are matched. If mercy is voided, however, only a fierce and fearsome judgment remains.

The situation is somewhat like a judge who sits in a courtroom and his own son is brought before him having committed a crime. The judge has to act in justice. If the son has committed the crime and there is no honorable way to pardon him, then the father as judge must sentence him to punishment. Although the father must act with justice, his heart has a greater desire to pardon him.

16

In the case with God as both our Father and our Judge, He has prepared a plan that provides for our pardon by having the punishment carried out on Yeshua. If we do not accept His provision for pardon, then we receive the punishment. God's role as a Father takes priority over His role as a Judge, but if we do not accept Him as Father, He has no choice but to act as Judge toward us. Mercy is greater than judgment, but when mercy is cheapened then judgment goes into operation.

When Yeshua was asked about the legal ramifications of divorce, He answered:

Mark 10:5-6
Because of the hardness of your heart he [Moses] wrote you this precept. But from the beginning of creation, God "made them male and female."

Because of the hardness of our hearts, God often has to approach us on a legal basis and with the threat of judgment. But that is not God's preference, nor is it His best way. The harder our hearts are, the more legal and punishment-oriented He has to become. The more cooperative our hearts are, the more He can reveal His true nature which is grace and love. God's nature of grace and love is a higher revelation than His nature of judgment and wrath.

GRACE AND LAW

God's original intention in marriage was simply for a man and woman to live in blissful harmony. Divorce laws were added because of the people's hardness of heart and lack of understanding of grace. The divorce laws are part of Scripture even though they are contrary to God's will. In general, the passages of judgment and wrath in Scripture are reluctantly God's will. Yes, they are expressing His divine will, but only in the circumstance in which He was forced to respond to evil.

When we sin, God punishes. When we repent, mercy is shown. When we obey, blessings come. God would rather bless. That is why He commands us to obey.

Galatians 3:19
What purpose then does the Law serve? It was added because of transgression...

I worked as the principal of a private Christian high school for several years. The only desire of the administration was that the students should maintain a cooperative and respectful attitude. In areas where the students could not maintain the positive attitudes, we had to add on rules and punishments to enforce a proper behavior. Rules and punishments can only enforce behavior modification; they cannot produce the correct heart attitude.

In areas where the students were cooperative, there was no need for rules. Where the attitude was less cooperative, the rules were added. Students whose hearts were wrong perceived the administration to be harsh and demanding. Students who were more perceptive saw that our only motivation was grace. If the students had merely been willing to be cooperative across the board, we could have done away with many of the rules.

Galatians 5:22-23
The fruit of the spirit is love, joy, peace, long-suffering, kindness, goodness, faithfulness, self-control. Against such there is no law.

If God could have His preference, there would be no judgment and no wrath. God appears to be hard to those who are hard themselves, but that is not the truth. As we are walking in the right attitude of grace, the laws of judgment do not affect us. Divorce laws do not affect me if I love my wife. Stealing laws do not affect me if my needs are already met and I do not steal. When our hearts are right with God, He has no motivation to act in wrath unless He is forced into it. The more our hearts are right toward Him, the more we will see Him as He really is: the God of both love and holiness.

Psalm 18:25-26
With the merciful You will show Yourself merciful. With a blameless man You will show Yourself blameless; With the pure You will show Yourself pure; and with the devious You will show Yourself shrewd.

To the meek, He will show Himself to be merciful. To the stubborn, He will show Himself to be hard. But He prefers the former.

GOD LOVES EVEN SINNERS

When God originally created us in Adam, He saw great potential value in us as a creature made in His image. Unfortunately, we ruined that potential value through sin. Every human being is of infinite preciousness to God. It is not God's will that any person should perish (II Peter 3:9; I Timothy 2:4). Even people who have not accepted their salvation in Messiah Yeshua are of great worth to God. God loves everyone in the world (John 3:16).

It was because of this love that He sent Yeshua to the cross. God loved us before we accepted His salvation, and before we loved Him. While we were still sinners, God loved us (Romans 5:8). Even sinners are loved of God despite His anger at them because of their sin.

Some people believe that God brings both good and bad upon people indiscriminately. That is not true. His only desire is to bring good things to us. "But does not God bring both sunshine and rain, good and evil?" some might ask.

Matthew 5:44-45

Love your enemies, bless those who curse you, do good to those who hate you, and pray for those who spitefully use you and persecute you, that you may be sons of your Father in heaven; for He makes the sun rise on the evil and the good, and sends rain on the just and the unjust.

Rain here does not represent bad things. Rain in the Middle East is the greatest source of blessing. The meaning of this passage is not that God brings both good and bad things on people, but that He brings good things on both good and bad people. God loves even the worst of sinners. He offers us salvation even while we are spitting in His face. He offers us forgiveness at the same time that He is furious with us because of our sins.

ARE YOU WORTHLESS?

What is so exasperating in the light of God's high estimation of our value as human beings is that we often turn away from that high evaluation and defile ourselves before Him. The picture is not that of a man who has a wife that he does not care about, but rather one of a man who has a wife that he is intensely in love with who betrays him.

Proverbs 11:22

As a ring of gold in a swine's snout, so is a lovely woman who lacks discretion.

It is not that the woman in this proverb is of little worth. The very thing that makes the situation so evil is that she is ruining her potential. She is a lovely masterpiece that has been defiled. It is her very worth and beauty that makes what she has done so horrible. To deface a masterpiece original oil painting in a museum is much more appalling than to destroy a cheap copy of one in a magazine. God sees us as gold; we have acted like dirt. God sees us a beautiful woman; we have acted like pigs.

If God did not care about us so much, He would not be so incensed at our sin. It is the very height of how precious we are to God that makes our turning away from Him so grotesque. If wallowing in sin is perverse in the light of God's love for us, so is it equally wrong to wallow in feelings of worthlessness and unworthiness when God has placed such a high value upon us.

Whenever you are thinking that you are worthless, it immediately contradicts the Word of God. The Bible says that you are of great value (Luke 12:7). Our value in and of ourselves is zero. However, we have value because God sees value in us. He has creative ability to develop something of worth inside us.

A friend of mine once had a hobby of buying old jalopies and fixing them up. He would essentially rebuild them totally from scratch, from the inside out. Then he would resell them for a profit as restored antique cars. One time an old car that he planned to fix up was brought into the garage. I asked him how much it was worth.

He replied, *"You don't understand. This car isn't worth anything. It is a piece of junk. The value is all inside my head, in my imagination. In my creativity and skills, I can make something out of it that is beautiful, stylish and worth money."*

So it is with God and us. Without His creativity we are without worth. Yet in His love, He sees potential in us that He can make something beautiful and worthwhile out of our lives. We have to trust Him and let Him do His work in us.

At one of our staff meetings, we did a team building exercise, where we would tell a good quality we see in one another. Someone said of me, *"You look at us in a way that you see worth and potential that we don't even see in ourselves."* Seeing God's destiny and potential in others is part of **"faith working through love" (Galatians 5:6).**

SAVED FROM SIN

Sin is what ruins people. All people have sinned, and that is why all people have fallen prey to death and destruction. We recognize sin; we identify it, and we call it what it is. Sometimes it is necessary to clobber someone with the fact that he is a sinner to break him out of a spiritual deception, as Yeshua had to do with the Pharisees. It is necessary to rebuke religious hypocrisy publicly so that others will not be taken captive by it (Matthew 23). The central thrust of the gospel is that Yeshua is the Lamb of God who takes away the sin of the world.

This is the mistake that Jonah made in his attitude toward preaching to Nineveh. Jonah expected God to annihilate the Ninevites. He was disappointed, even irritated, that God did not do so (Jonah 4:1). Jonah missed the point that even in the most severe rebuke of sin, God's only desire is to rescue and restore the people.

Abraham understood this principle. When God went to destroy Sodom and Gomorrah, He allowed Abraham to enter into covenant dialogue to dissuade Him from doing so. Abraham knew that God's ultimate desire was to save the people of Sodom and Gomorrah, not to destroy them.

James and John experienced a wrong attitude when they saw the Samaritans reject Yeshua.

> **Luke 9:54-56**
> **And when His disciples James and John saw this, they said, "Lord, do You want us to command fire to come down from Heaven and consume them, just as Elijah did?" But He turned and rebuked them, and said, "You do not know what manner of spirit you are of. For the Son of Man did not come to destroy men's lives but to save them."**

They thought they were exercising righteous indignation, but they had slipped into the subtle trap of condemning others.

They did not realize that they had done it. They did not know what spirit they were of. Many preachers are not even aware that they are preaching condemnation. Preaching is to be done in the spirit of desiring to bless and purify people. The purpose of preaching is to always build others up and rescue them from the snares of death and sin.

TO LOVE IS TO EDIFY

To love someone is to build someone up.

I Corinthians 8:1
Knowledge puffs up, but love edifies.

The definition of love is to edify someone. Edify means to build up or strengthen a person from within. The best way to edify a person is to speak words of revelation to him so that he will be strengthened and encouraged on the inside.

The essence of prayer is to pray for someone to be strengthened on the inside (Ephesians 3:16). The essence of preaching is to speak words anointed of the Holy Spirit to empower the hearer to succeed.

Ephesians 4:29
Let no corrupt word proceed out of your mouth, but what is good for necessary edification, that it may impart grace to the hearers.

Every time a person hears a sermon, he should leave stronger than when he came in. Every time you speak to a person, he should go away from you closer to God than when he met you. Every word we speak, in prayer or in preaching or in conversation, should strengthen those to whom it was directed.

HELL IS REAL

Some people say that hell is not real, that it is only figurative, and that people will not really experience pain for eternity. That is a lie. Yeshua went out of his way to describe the torments of hell in the most physical and realistic terms possible.

How would you try to communicate to people that hell is absolutely real and not figurative in any way? Yeshua said that hell is so bad that it would be better to physically tear your eyes out of your body or tear off your arms and legs than to be thrown into the fires of hell (Matthew 5:29-30; 18:8-9; Mark 9:42-48). He said that people scream and yell and gnash their teeth under the pain (Matthew 13:42,50) and that it would be better to lose everything in this life rather than to be damned (Matthew 16:26). He said that people are completely aware and conscious of their pain (Luke 16:23-25). They try to repent and desire to escape but it is too late (Matthew 25:11). In fact there is a barrier and gulf set up so that no one can cross from hell to heaven of from heaven to hell (Luke 16:26).

God does not want people to go to hell. In fact it was not designed for humans at all but for the devil and the other rebellious angels. But any person who refuses to align himself with God has aligned himself knowingly or unknowingly with the devil and will go with the devil to his judgment and punishment (Revelation 21:8).

That is why we feel such a compulsion to go out into all the world and tell about the gospel. That is exactly what Yeshua commanded us to do. We beg you; we implore you, to be reconciled with God through Yeshua. Nothing that this world could possibly offer is worth the torment of spending eternity in hell.

PREACHING RIGHTEOUSNESS

We do not dismiss sin or deny that it exists. Modern philosophers and so-called "new" thinkers say that people are all right the way they are, that people are not in need of divine forgiveness, and that guilt is just a psychological phenomenon to be ignored. That is preposterous. We are not dismissing sin. On the contrary, we are preaching the antidote to sin, which is repentance and forgiveness. We are not emphasizing the problem of sin but rather the solution to it. Yeshua told us to preach repentance and the forgiveness of sins.

Luke 24:47
...repentance and remission of sins should be preached in His name to all nations.

Dismissing sin is secular humanism. Preaching only about sin is religious condemnation. Preaching repentance and remission of sins is the gospel. The remission or the getting rid of the sin is what we are concentrating on.

When Paul said that all men have sinned and fallen short of the glory of God (Romans 3:23), he was actually making a point about righteousness, not about sin. He was preaching that righteousness has now been made available to all men freely. Righteousness is the antidote to sin and is available to anyone who has sinned. Since all men have sinned, that righteousness is available to all. It was in the context of preaching free faith righteousness that Paul was identifying the fact that all men have sinned.

Romans 3:21-25
The righteousness of God... is revealed... through faith in Yeshua the Messiah to all and on all who believe. For there is no difference; for all have sinned and fall short of the glory of God, being justified freely by His grace... because in His forbearance,

God had passed over the sins that were previously committed.

From God's point of view, the problem of sin has been dealt with. God has already accepted Yeshua's substitutionary death for us. God has already forgiven all of us before we realize it. The question is not whether we can get God to forgive us, but whether we will accept the forgiveness God has already given us. God on His part has unilaterally reconciled Himself to us. The question is only whether we will be reconciled to Him in return.

II Corinthians 5:18-20
> **...God who has reconciled us to Himself through Messiah Yeshua... God was in Messiah reconciling the world to Himself, not imputing their trespasses to them. We are ambassadors for Messiah, as though God were pleading through us: we implore you on Messiah's behalf, be reconciled to God.**

God has already forgiven you of your sins. He has already accepted Yeshua's substitution as a solution to sin. The problem with sin is that it keeps us away from returning to God to receive His grace. God has done away with the sin barrier. The only thing keeping you away from God is your unbelief. This is what we mean when we say the only thing keeping you away from God is your lack of belief in Yeshua: lack of belief that Yeshua has done away with the barrier between you and God.

The door has been opened. The death and resurrection of Messiah Jesus blew a hole in the wall; it opened the door. We are begging you to make the decision to repent and walk through that open door. One of the problems with sin is that it destroys your faith to walk through that door of grace. When you sin, your conscience is poisoned by guilt. When you sin, you re-erect the barrier, even though Yeshua had to die to have that sin barrier torn down.

We have to identify sin for what it is because sin brings you into deception and bondage. The barrier of sin has been torn down. We preach that righteousness through the blood of Yeshua is being freely offered. Preaching righteousness engenders faith to come forward and receive forgiveness. We preach righteousness so that you will be able to receive righteousness.

Often we hear people say that they have to stay away from fellowship because they have sinned. That is foolish. We do not reject sinners. Repent, ask for forgiveness and come back. The fact that you have sinned does not prevent us from loving you. We will forgive you. If we are gracious enough to forgive each other's sins, certainly God is. Repentance means to stop sinning and make a commitment to obey God.

Righteousness is right standing with God. Return to Him and receive your right standing with God. That is righteousness. It takes faith to receive it. That is righteousness by faith. That is what we preach (Romans 10:6,8).

A TOUGH MESSAGE

If someone will not listen to God's offer of grace, he is under the condemnation of the law of perfect justice. If a person will not listen to the voice of love, love demands that we challenge and confront that person as hard as we can. The motive and spirit is always one of love, but the message may have to be tough.

It is said of a drowning person that if he will not cooperate with his rescuer, that the drowning person must be knocked out so that he can be dragged to shore. It is so urgent for us to help people escape from the eternal torment of hell that Yeshua said we should go out into the highways and byways and drag people into the kingdom of God (Luke 14:21,23).

Our role as evangelists is somewhat like a fireman who goes into a burning to pull people out of the flames. The world is falling apart. It is a burning building collapsing around the victims. People's situations are desperate, utterly without remedy, outside the salvation of Yeshua.

It is also important that people who will never receive the gospel be told the consequences and penalties of disobedience. Justice demands that even the most recalcitrant sinner be warned before he goes off into damnation. Even if he will not repent, he deserves the right of being warned and legally notified of what he is facing.

For example, the government may come up with drug rehabilitation centers, but unless young people are fully warned of the criminal charges connected with drug use, they will continue to use drugs. Clear notification and enforcement of criminal charges is a strong deterrent to sin. The fear of punishment is a primary method of changing people's attitudes and behaviors.

THE EFFECT OF SELF-IMAGE

We do not dismiss sin, nor do we use guilt manipulation. We rebuke sin and preach righteousness.

Proverbs 23:7
As a man thinks in his heart, so is he.

If a man sees himself as worthless, so will he be. If he thinks of himself as a sinner, he will act like one. A man's self-image must be changed from that of being a sinner to that of being a righteous child of God.

For example, there are many people who are putting great effort into staying on a diet but never seem to be able to lose weight. No matter how hard a person tries to diet, if he sees himself as a glutton, he will not be able to maintain a weight loss. In addition to the discipline of dieting, the person must gain a positive self-image in order to succeed. A person will become outwardly that which he sees himself to be on the inside.

It has become an effective practice for Olympic athletes to watch video of current world-record holders for the purpose of programming themselves with a mental image of victory. The best athletes are those who have an image of themselves winning the prize, making the goal or crossing the finish line. The same principle works in reverse.

Matthew 5:28
Whoever looks at a woman to lust for her has already committed adultery with her in his heart.

What a person thinks in his heart, he is accountable for in the eyes of the Lord. Who a person is in his heart is who he really is. As this principle works in the negative in the case of adultery, so it can also work in the positive.

A person who has an inner self-image as a winner will act like a winner. A person who sees himself as a good father will be one. A person who sees himself as an adulterer will be one. In fact, Yeshua said that a person who committed murder or adultery in his heart has virtually done it already (Matthew 5:22; I John 3:15).

A person who sees himself as a righteous child of God will act like one. If your self-image is modeled on Yeshua, then you will become more and more like Him. The person that you see yourself to be in your heart is who you are.

There are two ways to lose all consciousness of sin. One way is to become so hardened in sin that your conscience has become calloused and insensitive to sin's negative effects. The other way is to become so transformed in your own self-image by what Yeshua has done for you that you become distanced from any orientation to sin. You become dead to sin and alive to righteousness (Romans 6:11). Sin becomes foreign to you; you lose all consciousness of it. Guilt, defeat and self-condemnation are purged out of you (Hebrews 9:14; 10:2).

The first way is the lowest level of life; the second is the highest. The first way is damnation; the second is ultimate salvation. The first way is the road to hell; the second is the path of righteousness (Psalm 23:3).

Telling a born again believer that he is a sinner and is unworthy causes him to see himself that way. That line of thinking will thereby cause him to remove himself from his place of right standing before God. Thinking that one is a sinner and unworthy can have virtually the same effect as if the person had actually sinned and acted in an unworthy manner. Self-condemnation is the flip side of committing sin. Thinking of yourself as unworthy and worthless has virtually the same result in its effect on your relationship to God as if you had sinned.

PHYSICAL WORTH

In what ways are you worthwhile? First of all, physically, as a biological creation, you are a work of marvelous ingenuity. The one hundred thirty-ninth chapter of Psalms speaks of the wondrous design of the human body.

> **Psalm 139:14-15**
> **I will praise You, for I am fearfully and wonderfully made... My frame was not hidden from You, when I was made in secret, and skillfully wrought in the lowest parts of the earth.**

You are a biological miracle. Your physical body is a masterpiece. The infinite complexities of how you were made and put together are awe-inspiring. The mere fact that you exist is a miracle. Even on the level of who you are physically, you are exquisitely special. Of course, you yourself, as a spiritual being, are much more important than your mere physical frame. But if your body is so special, how much more so are you, as the person who inhabits it?

The vast number of individual operations that take place in your body every second is staggering. An ancient Jewish prayer, said upon rising in the morning, states, "Blessed are You, O Lord, our God, who has fashioned man in wisdom and created in him passages upon passages, vessels upon vessels. If even one of these be opened or one of them be closed, it would not be possible to exist or stand before You." Each function of the body, no matter how insignificant it seems, is miraculous.

Think about the wondrous design of the body that God has given you to live in. What does the evidence of that design say about how much God loves you? All human bodies at this time have been degraded by sin and death. This degraded state of the human body we call "the flesh." In the resurrection, righteous people will receive new and glorious bodies. But even in the present degraded state, we can see evidence of God's design.

CROWN OF CREATION

The Bible says that the heavens show forth the handiwork of God (Psalm 19). The starry expanse above us is magnificent. The seas are vast and powerful. All of creation, from the tiniest molecular particle to the hugeness of the galaxies, is wondrous.

God made everything in creation. In five days He completed all the magnificent work of the physical universe. He stepped back, considered it, and pronounced His appraisal of it: "Good!" Then He made you, and His appraisal was "Very Good!" (Genesis 1:31). All of creation without you is good; all of creation with you is very good. You are the crown of His creation. All of creation pales in comparison to you. You are magnificently and uniquely made in God's image.

Adam and Eve were the crown of God's creation. They were made in His image. As descendants of Adam we bear that image. When Adam and Eve rebelled against God, that image was horridly disfigured. But even as fallen human beings, marred as the image of God in us may be, we still bear the remnant of His likeness. When we come to believe in Yeshua, the image of God within our spirit is restored. If Adam and Eve were the crown of God's creation, how much more so are we His crown when we are recreated spiritually in the image of Yeshua. In Him we reclaim our position as the sons of God.

YESHUA DIED FOR YOU

If God could have blotted out all of creation to save one more human being, He would have done it. One soul is of infinite value to God. You, as one person, are of more importance to God than all of creation. God loved you so much that He gave His only Son, Yeshua, so that you could have life. God gave up the best that He had to benefit you. If no one else in the whole world would have accepted salvation, Yeshua would have gone to the cross for just you alone.

According to natural evidence, Yeshua had no way of knowing if anyone would accept salvation. He exercised His faith on behalf of mankind and believed that many would come to the knowledge of the truth. But in the natural, it looked doubtful that even His disciples would believe it. Even after the resurrection, there was no guarantee that His disciples would accept Him.

Matthew 28:17
And when they [the disciples] saw Him, they worshiped Him; but some doubted.

Yeshua died for you because He loved you. He had no assurance that anyone would accept the gospel. It was a unilateral act of faith on His part even if no one would have accepted it; He still would have given His life to offer us salvation. It was a risky matter, and Yeshua took the ultimate risk for us.

God says that you are of great worth. The world system tells you that you are not. Scriptures declare that you are of great value to God. Religious condemnation portrays God as an ogre telling you that you are no good.

II Corinthians 5:21

For He [God] made Him [Yeshua] who knew no sin to be sin for us, that we might become the righteousness of God in Him.

In Yeshua we become righteous. Yeshua died for us to show us how precious we are to God. He exchanges our sinfulness for His righteousness. His righteousness is imputed and transferred to us. We all sin, yet in Yeshua we are changed into being righteous. We are more than just forgiven sinners. We are forgiven sinners who have now become the righteousness of God in Yeshua.

POSITIVE SELF-IMAGE

The devil's work is to besmirch the glorious image of God in you. God's work is to restore that image in you. God desires to manifest His divine nature in us. The devil's method is to condemn you and suppress you from returning to God's glory. Yeshua became sin for you so that you could be transformed into the righteousness of God (II Corinthians 5:21). So be transformed. Receive your righteousness and be righteous. Come to your senses (I Corinthians 15:34). Wake up out of the pig pen of sin and a filthy self-image. Return to your heavenly Father like the prodigal son and put on the finest robes of sonship (Luke 15:17,22). Have faith and confidence in His love for you.

If Yeshua died for us on the cross so that we could become the righteousness of God, then to accept His sacrifice is to accept ourselves as the righteousness of God. To believe in Yeshua is to consider yourself to be the righteousness of God. If you do not accept yourself as having been made the righteousness of God, then you have not fully believed in what Yeshua has done for you.

Proverbs 28:1
The righteous are bold as a lion.

If we accept Yeshua's sacrifice for us, we must consider ourselves righteous. If we are righteous, then we should act like it. If the righteous are bold as a lion, then we should act as bold as a lion. Boldness is exactly the character quality that the early believers in Yeshua prayed to receive (Acts 4:29). So be bold.

Some of us, if we saw a little bird get hit by a car, would have great compassion on it. That is fine. But then we think more of that bird than we do of ourselves. "God cares about this little bird," we say with one breath; and "God does not care about me," we say with the next. That is absurd. You are of more value than five sparrows, nay, more than a universe full of them.

II Corinthians 4:15
All things are for your sakes...

All things are for you. All of creation, all of redemption, all of Scriptures, and all of God's actions are for you. That is good news.

CHAPTER 2
WHO YOU REALLY ARE

From God's side of sending this good news, He is saying, "I love you." From our side of receiving this message, we hear, "You are special." The receiving side of God's statement that He loves us is for us to grasp the revelation that we are special in His eyes. He gives; we receive. He loves; we become the object of that love. He speaks; we become what He says we are.

The more you pray for someone, the more you grow to love that person. As you intercede, you begin to walk in that person's shoes and to see from his perspective. The more you love someone, the more you want the best for him. The more you want the best for that person, the more you want for him to grasp a blossoming revelation of who he is in God's sight.

Catching the revelation of your infinite potential in Yeshua is the best thing that can happen to you. Knowing who you are in Messiah is one of the most important revelations of New Testament prayer. I pray that you would catch a revelation of who you are in Messiah Jesus. The apostle Paul prayed that:

> *Ephesians 1:18-19*
> **...the eyes of your understanding being enlightened; that you may know what is the hope of His calling, may know what is the hope of His calling, what are the riches of the glory of His inheritance in the saints,**

and what is the exceeding greatness of His power toward us who believe...

Begin to see who you are in Messiah. The unfolding of the revelation of the New Covenant inside you contains the unfolding of the revelation of who you are in Yeshua. You could give someone a million dollars, and it would be spent. You could pour a dump-truck load of blessings on top of someone, and he could walk out from under it. Nothing on the outside will work. The only thing that will do any permanent good is to get inside a person the revelation of who he is in the Messiah.

Can you get a revelation of what God is doing on the inside of you? Of what His destiny is for you? Of what He has called you to be? Of His divine nature growing inside you? Knowing who you are in Messiah Jesus and who He is in you is a key to the New Covenant.

The more you pray for someone to see this revelation, the more you will begin to see it for him. The more you pray for someone, the more you will see how precious that person is before God. The more you pray, the more you will see how gloriously special each and every person is to God. It is beautiful. Through faith in Yeshua, God is creating something pure, holy and glorious inside all of us who believe.

THE MASTERPIECE

The new "you" that Scripture is talking about is the new spirit person on the inside. That inner person is created as a separate work of God, distinct from the time that you were physically born. This second act of creation starts to take place in your life the moment you receive Yeshua into your heart as your personal Lord and Messiah. This second act of creation is a masterpiece of God's artistry.

Ephesians 2:10
For we are His workmanship, created in Messiah Yeshua for good works, which God prepared beforehand that we should walk in them.

You are God's workmanship, His craftsmanship. The voice of condemnation is telling you that you are no good and that you are worthless. God says, "You are My work of art. You are My masterpiece. You are the apple of My eye" (Zechariah 2:8). You are the center of the target that God's love is aimed at.

If you have been spiritually reborn, the you that you are now is not the same you that was born in your mother's womb. That old you is part of the person that has passed away. You are a new person. If you have received the revelation of God's Spirit, the real you is the part that was recreated. This second act of creation is as distinct as when God created the heavens and the earth. This second birth is as distinct as when you were conceived in your mother's womb. The state of the universe was as different after the moment when God raised Yeshua from the dead as it was after the moment when God said, "Let there be light." The state of mankind in the eyes of God is different since the moment of the resurrection.

II Corinthians 5:17
Therefore, if anyone is in Messiah, he is a new creation; old things have passed away; behold all things have become new.

That old part of you has passed away. In God's sight, it does not count. He is accounting you as a righteous new creation. The you that was started at the moment of new birth is perfect and pure. That new you was created in righteousness and true holiness (Ephesians 4:24). The new you that is the real you is made out of the same substance, the same inner essence, as God Himself. You are made "of" His Spirit. You are made out of the same stuff that the inside of God is made of. As God breathed into Adam biological breath, so has He breathed into you His own spiritual life (John 20:22). You are born of God.

GOD IS A GIVER

To believe is to receive. The act of believing is an act of receiving.

Mark 11:24
...whatever things you ask when you pray, believe that you receive them, and you will have them.

If you are unwilling to receive, then you do not believe. God is a giver. If we are to cooperate with Him and obey Him, we must receive. God is completely unselfish. He is not out to get something from us or to take from us. His motivation is to give to us.

The whole universe runs on a system centered on the fact that God is a giver. The system based on God's giving nature is called grace. God wants the universe to operate according to grace.

Our response to God's grace is faith. Grace is God's giving. Faith is our receiving. If the system of grace is at work, then we must operate by faith.

Romans 4:16
Therefore it is of faith that it might be according to grace...

God is good, and God is a giver. God has given us all that He has. He has given us the best that He has. He has even given us His only begotten Son (John 3:16).

Romans 8:32
He who did not spare His own Son... how shall He not with Him also freely give us all things.

If God has already given us His Son, how much more so will He give us anything else that is good? If He has already given us what is most expensive, obviously He will give us all the things of lesser worth. If God is willing to spend a thousand dollars on you, He must be willing to spend a hundred. If God was willing to give Yeshua for us, there obviously is not anything that He would not give.

The degree to which God is gracious to us and gives to us is unfathomable to the natural human mind. It takes a special impartation of the Spirit of God into our hearts even to catch a glimpse of all the good things God wants to give us.

> **I Corinthians 2:12**
> **Now we have received... the Spirit who is from God that we might know the things that have been freely given to us by God.**

One of the reasons that we need to receive the Holy Spirit is to understand how much God has given to us. Without the Holy Spirit we cannot see that God's true nature is that of a giver. We need the help of the Holy Spirit to grasp the fact that God actually wants to give to us, that it is the desire of His own free will to do it.

God's nature is to give. What He gives He gives freely. God wants us to be cheerful givers (II Corinthians 9:7) because that is the way He is. God Himself is a cheerful giver. God commands us to be cheerful givers because He was that way before we were. He does not command us to be cheerful givers because He wants to get something out of us.

GOD IS GOOD

The all-powerful God who created the universe just happens to be purely and wholly good. And it is a good thing for us that He is. He is one hundred percent benevolent. Did you ever think that He did not have to be so perfectly good? There is nothing we could have done about it if God was an all-powerful but selfish being. He just as well could have been a tyrant who was corrupted by his absolute power. He could have been an all-powerful being who desired to have many slaves and servants worshipping Him and waiting on Him. That is the way most human rulers have been. God could have been completely justice-oriented with no inclination toward mercy or benevolence. Thank God that He is the way He is. Thank God that He is completely pure, holy and good.

Romans 8:31
If God is for us, who can be against us?

God is for us. He is on our side. Since He is for us, there is no force of opposition that can overcome us. God is not against you. He is for you. He wants you to succeed in every area of your life. When we accept God's benevolent aid, our victory is assured.

WALKING IN VICTORY

If you are a new creation, then recognize the fact that God does not want you to be living in moral or spiritual defeat. That is only logical. If you are God's masterpiece, then He does not want you to be living under the thumb of death and debt; He does not want you under the thumb of curses and disease; He does not want you under the thumb of physical pain, emotional stress or mental confusion. If you are made out of the very inside of God, then He must desire to have you walk in the same victory and triumph that He does (I Corinthians 15:57; II Corinthians 2:14). God's own nature is one of victory. Therefore His nature within us compels us toward victory as well.

God wants us to live as He lives. He lives not only in moral purity but also in abundance of life. We are told to pray that

God's will would come to pass on earth the same way it does in heaven (Matthew 6:10). But in heaven, the people live in prosperity and joy. The streets are paved with gold (Revelation 21:21). God wants that heavenly lifestyle to be spread across the planet. In the days of King Solomon, there was so much gold that silver was counted as worthless (I Kings 10:21). Instead of having paper throwaway plates, they had silver ones. Moral excellence includes peace and physical health. Godliness comprises not only morality but also the resourcefulness to be successful in every arena of life (II Peter 1:3; Joshua 1:8).

MYSTERY OF SUFFERING

While it is not the purpose of God to cause us to suffer, suffering is a necessary part of the process of following God's will. Like the Messiah Himself, we have to deny ourselves and take up our crosses every day in order to follow after Him (Luke 9:23). The goal is to be like Him. But as He suffered, so will we suffer in this world.

If the world was already perfect and all the people in it perfect, there would be no suffering. That will be the case at the end (Revelation 21:4). In the meantime, there is evil in the world. The more one endeavors to be righteous, the more the evil in the world will react against him and attack him. Therefore, the more one is righteous, the more he will suffer.

God's goal is to give us His eternal love, glory and holiness. There is no way to obtain such high goals without suffering in the process. - As the saying goes in the sports world, "No pain, no gain." The goal in sports is to win the gold medal. God has spiritual gold to give us, yet there is suffering to go through in the training process.

II Corinthians 1:4-8
...who comforts us in all our tribulation, that we may be able to comfort those who are in any tribulation...

> For as the sufferings of Christ abound in us, so
> our consolation also abounds through Christ. ...
> enduring the same sufferings which we also suffer. As
> you are partakers of the suffering, so also will you
> partake of the consolation. We do not want you to
> be ignorant, brethren, of our tribulation... We were
> burdened beyond measure, above strength, so that we
> despaired even of life.

As we give ourselves to others in love, there is pain involved.
People hurt one another. Love involves pain. But the final
goal is the joy of intimacy and trust. One quality of love is
"longsuffering." One cannot develop the quality of longsuffering
without some suffering along the way.

> *I Peter 1:7*
> ...the genuineness of your faith, being much more
> precious than gold that perishes, though it is tested
> by fire...

> *I Peter 4:13*
> ...rejoice to the extent that you partake of Christ's
> sufferings, that when His glory is revealed, you may
> also be glad with exceeding joy.

Our faith is like gold; yet gold must be refined in a furnace. The
furnace is the suffering. It's the gold we want, not the furnace,
but the furnace is part of the process. Yeshua suffered first, then
entered His glory. To the degree that we share His sufferings, we
will also share His glory.

REDEEMED FROM WHAT?

The Bible is the story of the plan of redemption. Redemption
means that we have been bought back. If we have been redeemed,

we must have been bought back from a certain bad condition. We must have been bought back into something good that we once had previously. If mankind has fallen, the place where we fell from must have been higher and better than the place where we fell to. If we have been redeemed, then we must have been restored to that higher, better position we originally had.

We can catch a glimpse of that better lifestyle both in the Garden of Eden at the beginning of the Bible and in Heavenly Jerusalem at the end of the Bible. The place from which we fell is the place to which we are being restored. There was nothing evil or negative in the Garden; there will be nothing evil or negative in Paradise restored. By definition, anything that exists that is destructive and unwholesome is a product of the sin of man and the rebellion of the devil. By definition, anything that is negative and destructive is ultimately against God's will. The plan of salvation is to remove all the results of the Fall. God's will is to restore the lifestyle of Eden. And that is just a start. From there it will get even better.

Colossians 1:13-14
He has delivered us from the power of darkness and translated us into the kingdom of the Son of His love, in whom we have redemption.

God wants you to be free of any and every form of Satan's dominion. Satan's government is one of tyranny and evil. It causes you harm. God's government is one of benevolence and goodness. It brings you health. God is not out to hurt you. Whatever harms you is of the kingdom of Satan; whatever brings you wholeness is of the kingdom of God. If we are God's masterpiece, then He wants us to walk in the fullness of His blessings. His blessings are spiritual, holy and pure (Ephesians 1:3).

LACKING NOTHING

Whatever is good and wholesome God wants for you. God is the only source of good things. If there is anything that is good, it must have come from God. If there is anything that is not good, it cannot have come from God.

> **James 1:17**
> **Every good gift and every perfect gift is from above, and comes down from the Father of lights, with whom there is no variation or shadow of turning.**

This truth is black and white. There is no grey in the issue. All good things are from God. All bad things are from the devil. God wants you to have all good things.

> **Psalm 84:11**
> **No good thing will He withhold from those who walk uprightly.**

If there is a good thing, God wants you to have it. He is not the one holding back on you. The Lord does not want you to lack any good thing. The Lord acts as a shepherd to you to make sure you will not be in lack (Psalm 23:1; 34:10). He is your protector and your provider. God's very nature is one of a provider. One of His names is Jehovah Jireh, which means, "I am your provider" (Genesis 22:14). God will supply any and every one of our needs out of His heart of generosity (Philippians 4:19).

> **James 1:4**
> **But let patience have its perfect work, that you may be perfect and complete, lacking nothing.**

God wants you to be lacking nothing. God wants you to be perfectly whole and complete. He wants you to develop godly personality traits, such as patience, so that you can come to the point of lacking nothing. What a good God we have! Patience is one of the most mature character qualities of God, and by its very nature takes a long time to develop.

THE WHOLESOME SPIRIT

God's Spirit is one of wholesomeness. His Spirit always promotes health, life, wholeness, goodness, purity, positive attitudes, and so on. The very nature of a demonic spirit is self-destructive to the person whom it is influencing.

In the area of Gadarenes, Yeshua met a man with an unclean spirit. Look how the unclean spirit affected the man:

> **Mark 5:5**
> **And always, night and day, he was in the mountains and in the tombs, crying out and cutting himself with stones.**

When a person sins, his conscience tells him that he has done wrong. If he does not know how to appropriate repentance and forgiveness, he will grow to feel more and more guilty. The guilt will make him want to punish himself, and that self-destructive attitude is grounds for the influence of an unclean spirit.

The man at the Gadarenes was cutting himself with stones. An unclean spirit is always self-destructive. The Holy Spirit is never self-destructive. When the Holy Spirit set the man free, he was described as:

> **Mark 5:15**
> **...sitting and clothed and in his right mind.**

The Holy Spirit made him whole again. That is always the case. God's will is always for you to be made whole. God wants your mind renewed, your body healed, your family at peace, and your finances prospering. Under the influence of the demonic spirit, the man was torn, cutting himself and doing unclean activities. Under the influence of the Holy Spirit, he was made whole. Everything unwholesome was taken away.

You can discern an unclean spirit because it bears an unwholesome attitude. You can discern the Holy Spirit because He always guides you into wholesome activities. The Holy Spirit is the spirit of wholesomeness. The Holy Spirit is the Wholesome Spirit.

Taking drugs could not be of the Holy Spirit because it causes brain damage. Sexual perversion could not be of the Holy Spirit because it is unclean. Self-destructive attitudes are not of God because they hurt you and tear you down. Worried thoughts, negativity, resentment, self-hatred, lust and greed cannot be of God because they cause destruction in your life.

POSITIVE THINKING

There has been much discussion as to whether positive thinking and a positive mental attitude are Biblical concepts. Much attention has been given to these topics in the secular arena. We as believers do not have to copy things found in the secular world. If anything, the positive motivation techniques found in the world are an imitation of the faith and hope principles found in the Bible. We are not copying them; they are copying us. Just because there is a counterfeit to what we are doing, there is no reason for us to discontinue the real thing.

We have the only source of genuine hope and positive thinking: the life and love of God. Let's face it: without Yeshua there is no reason whatsoever to have an optimistic attitude of any sort. But with Him, we have cause to rejoice and be full of good cheer no matter how dark the circumstances. The world is craving for a true, positive solution. They need it desperately. We have it. Let's let our light shine.

Matthew 5:16
Let your light so shine before men, that they may see your good works and glorify your Father in heaven.

Optimism is not a bad thing from a Biblical point of view. God often rebuked the children of Israel in the wilderness because of their murmuring and complaining. Murmuring and complaining is a negative attitude. Only Joshua and Caleb maintained an optimistic attitude in the face of contrary circumstances. They received God's approval; the others did not.

Our optimism is more than just a positive mental attitude. It is a powerful spiritual force. The force of joy comes from God through the human spirit to overcome negative situations. It takes courage to be joyful when the circumstances around you are grim.

James 1:2
My brethren, count it all joy when you fall into various trials...

The power of joy is there to help you overcome the trial. Joy does not come from the mind; it comes from the heart. We go beyond positive thinking. We have super-positive thinking. We have overcoming faith.

CHANGING YOUR FOCUS

Our joy and optimism is not based on a mere psychological perception, but on the solid rock foundation of biblical truth. We are instructed to live our lives continuously in positive hope and faith.

I Corinthians 13:13
And now abide faith, hope, love, these three...

We are to consider every situation in light of the fact that Yeshua has rescued us from all evil. Others may be optimistic by being naïve and gullible. But our optimism is based on fact: Yeshua has been raised from the dead. That fact changes our outlook on everything.

II Corinthians 2:14
Thanks be to God who always leads us in triumph in Messiah...

When people ask us how we are, we can respond, "Triumphant." We are not triumphant due to circumstances or emotions, but due to the reality of what Yeshua has done for us in the spiritual realm. Yeshua's victory over sin, sickness and Satan is more real than any outward circumstance. We base our thoughts and words not on how we feel, but on what we know to be true in Scriptures.

For example, suppose I were to give you a free gift of a million dollars. On our way out of the bank from depositing the check in your account, you stub your toe on the door. A moment later on the street, a friend stops you and asks you how you are. I am standing right beside you. What do you say? Do you say, "I've had a terrible day. I just stubbed my toe." Or do you say, "Wonderful! My dear friend just gave me a million dollars!"?

If you respond negatively, you will have offended me and will have been unappreciative of the gift. If you respond positively, you are overlooking a present, temporary physical discomfort to focus on a greater spiritual truth. That is how we speak positively.

Romans 8:18
For I consider the sufferings of this present time are not worthy to be compared with the glory which shall be revealed in us.

We do not say that the sufferings of this world do not exist. But when we compare them with the glorious things God has done for us, they do not seem so large and ominous anymore. In fact, they hardly seem worth mentioning. So, we choose not to focus on them. We are more than conquerors despite the efforts of the world to annihilate us (Romans 8:39). Faith gives us the victory, not feelings (I John 5:4). We make a quality decision not to speak of what the enemy is doing to attack us, but of what Yeshua is doing to glorify us. We choose to consider what Yeshua is doing. We focus on Him, despite the circumstances, and run our race with joy (Hebrews 12:1-3).

CHOOSE BLESSINGS

Cursing is negative and destructive. Blessings are positive and enriching. The great Curse entered and spread across this planet at the Fall of Adam. In Yeshua we are delivered from that curse (Galatians 3:13). That curse affected every possible area of life; it poisoned the whole of mankind's existence. In Yeshua the destructive forces that entered into every possible area of life are reversed. God wants us to be blessed, not cursed. The state of the world is the curse; the message of the gospel is the blessing. The blessing overrides the curse. The power of the Good News overcomes all the negative forces in the world. Anyone who receives the Good News is an overcomer (I John 5:4-5).

> *Deuteronomy 30:19*
> **...I have set before you life and death, blessing and cursing; therefore choose life, that both you and your descendants may live...**

God wants to bless you, not curse you. In fact, He commands us to make the decision of our wills to receive His blessings. We are to purpose in our hearts to reject all the elements of the curse that exist on the earth. The gospel is the message of the blessing: it is the message that the blessing promised to Abraham for the benefit of mankind has finally overcome and destroyed the curse. The curse is obliterated by the blessing. Yeshua is the incarnation of the promise of the blessing that was to come. To preach the gospel is to proclaim that the blessing has won and is now available to all men. He who receives the gospel gets the blessings; he who refuses to receive has not believed. To believe the gospel is to receive the blessings (Mark 16:15-18).

The same pattern is true for every matter of spiritual life, from the smallest detail to the grandest destiny. To reject God's gracious offer of blessing is to be without hope or God in the world (Ephesians 2:12). It is to face eternity with all positive elements removed. It is utter desolation and unending damnation. Damnation is the ultimate outcome of rejecting God's grace. Refusing to receive God's blessings in the everyday affairs of life is the same pattern in miniature of rejecting eternal salvation. A lifestyle of self-condemnation is a temporal nugget of eternal damnation. Who wants it? Get rid of it.

The third chapter of Galatians indicates that the gospel is the same as the promises made to Abraham.

Galatians 3:8-9,16
The Scripture... preached the gospel to Abraham beforehand, saying, "In you all the nations shall be blessed." So then those who are of faith are blessed with believing Abraham... Now to Abraham and his Seed were the promises made.

The positive promises of the Old Covenant are the gospel. A true Bible-oriented Judaism and a truth faith-filled Christianity would be the same thing. God said, "I promise to bless you." That is the gospel; the gospel is good news.

THE COMPLETION OF GOD

God wants us to have the fullness of blessing. God Himself is the greatest blessing. Therefore, God wants us to have the fullness of Himself. If we have the fullness of Him inside us, then in a certain way we are the fullness of Him.

> *Ephesians 3:19*
> **...that you may be filled with all the fullness of God.**

> *Ephesians 1:22-23*
> **And He [God] put all things under His [Yeshua's] feet, and gave Him to be head over all things to the church, which is His body, the fullness of Him who fills all in all.**

You may have to blink your eyes and reread those verses a few times. As His body, we are the fullness of God. We who have received God's grace form a body of people. Yeshua is the head of this body of people. This body of people is filled with God's own Spirit. God's Spirit is His fullness. That is how we are filled with all the fullness of God. This body of people is filled with the indwelling presence of the glory of God. Therefore, we as a people should be glorious, radiating His glory.

The same Spirit that was in Yeshua is in us. The Messiah-anointing is the fullness of God; it contains all the treasures of divine wisdom and knowledge (Colossians 1:27; 2:3,9). In some mysterious marvelous way, we complete God (Ephesians 1:23) and He completes us (Colossians 2:10). God is our dwelling place and we are His dwelling place. God's glory was not meant to dwell in a pillar of cloud, but in us. We are God's body, the extension of His spiritual presence on this physical planet. We are the temple of the Holy Spirit (I Corinthians 6:19).

God is obviously complete without any dependence on us. He is complete and independent on His own. It is in His relationship to us that He is incomplete without us. For example, I am a complete person of myself, but in another sense I am incomplete without my wife. She completes me in our relationship as husband and wife. I am a complete person, but in my role as a father, I am incomplete without my children. God is omnipotent, holy and distinct from you and me. But as the covenant-making God of Abraham, Isaac, and Jacob, He is completed through the relationship with His people. As Father God, He is completed through His family.

We are not God. That is blasphemy. That is New Age occultism and self-worship. But we are partakers of the divine nature (II Peter 1:4). We are not the vine, but we are the branches (John 15:5). The vine does not bear the fruit; the branch does. He has the life-giving sap; we are the place where the fruit grows.

THE REAL YOU

When we say that we are the righteousness of God, we are not referring to all human beings. Being the righteousness of God is available to any person, but it applies only to those people, scattered among every tribe and nation, who have been transformed on the inside by faith in the death and resurrection of the Messiah. These people are the new creation. They constitute a new line of people, spiritually descended from Yeshua even as the human race is physically descended from Adam. These inwardly transformed people have been reborn as a new race, a new species, a new family.

On the inside, then, we have become a new person. It is the new person that we are talking about when we refer to ourselves as the righteousness of God. The habits of the old, outward man are still there, hanging around as it were, in a state of passing away. The outer man is no longer what counts. We do not weigh or consider the old personality as important. We make the mental decision to consider it void. We reckon old habits as dead. We train ourselves to identify with the newly transformed inner man. We force ourselves, despite our emotional contradictions, to see ourselves as that new person and not the old.

Identifying with the new inner man is a key to having that inner transformation grow outward to revitalize our lives. In faith we focus on and identify ourselves with that new person on the inside. As we live according to that new nature, it grows. As we walk in our new Yeshua-like self-image, the old nature fades away. We speak and act out of our new creation nature, and we are transformed more and more into it. In Yeshua, we are forgiven, healed and raised up to new heights. Those inner realities are gradually taking over the rest of our lives. Identifying yourself as the new inner man is a key to living a life of victory.

[For your reference, we have provided a list of some of those scriptures which identify the real you as the new-creation, inner-person. They are found at the back of this book as an appendix. Please meditate on them.]

CHAPTER 3
THE DRAMA OF YOUR LIFE

If we are to become the glorious children of God, there must be a process through which we become glorified. That process is the unfolding drama. Behind every person's life is a dramatic story. There is a special history to everyone's life. Each person could have an exciting biography written about him. People love to hear testimonies of what has happened to others.

> **Romans 8:29-30**
> **For whom He foreknew, He also predestined to be conformed to the image of His Son, that He might be the firstborn among many brethren. Moreover, whom He predestined, these He also called; whom He called, these He also justified; and whom He justified, these He also glorified.**

God knew you before you were even born. The first stage of your life's testimony is that God "foreknew" you before any consciousness came into your own being. He knew your personality; He understood you. He knew who you were and what you were going to become before it happened. That says something about how precious you are. Eons before you were born, God knew all the ins and outs about you.

A PREDESTINED PLAN

God also had a design and plan for you. Stage two of your life is that God "predestined" you. Predestination refers to the moment you entered life on this planet. By the time you got here, there was already a prefigured plan for you that you did not even know about.

I remember during my wife's pregnancies how we would pray over our children while they were in the womb. We would dream dreams about their lives. We built up our expectancy for them before they were born. By the time they came out, we were already excited to see them. We had welcomed them in before they even knew we existed. We had all kinds of imaginary plans and hopes laid out for their future success. I would lay my hands on my wife's belly and speak to my preborn children, telling them that we loved them and that we were looking forward to them being a part of our family. We had a crib and a room and baby clothes all ready. We had plans for them before they were even born.

God is like that. He has plans for us before we are even born. His plans for us are for our well-being and success (Jeremiah 29:11). He is a Father plotting for our good. He knows us better than we know ourselves, and His plans for us are better than we could ever think up on our own behalf. The fact that He has these plans for your life is proof of how precious you are to Him.

Although God has a unique plan for every person's life, there is one element that is the same ultimate destiny for each of us. We are all "predestined to be conformed to the image of His Son, that He might be the firstborn among many brethren." Yeshua is portrayed as our elder brother in the Spirit. He is the pattern that we are to fit. We all have an inherent instinct on the inside that longs for us to be just like Jesus. God's plan for us is to be just like Yeshua. He is the key that unlocks our true innermost personality. The image of Yeshua is the mold that we are poured out of.

We were created in Adam originally to be the image of God. We are recreated in Yeshua ultimately to regain the image of God. Yeshua did not come to earth to prove He was the Son of God. He came to make you and me sons of God with Him. His miraculous ministry was not to emphasize the vast difference between Him and us, but to bring many of us as sons up into glory with Him (Hebrews 2:10). God is our Father. Yeshua is the firstborn Son, our older brother. We become part of the same divine family through faith in Yeshua.

MY TESTIMONY

I know that God has had a plan and a purpose for my life. During World War I, my Zeyda (grandfather) fled from Eastern Europe to America. Eastern Europe was falling apart. It was obvious that whole-scale Jewish communities were about to be decimated in the coming years. The family took my grandfather and said, "You escape. You survive. Live at all costs. Take the family name. Go to another country." They invested their hopes for future generations in him and sent him off with their prayers. My firstborn son is named after him. I am named after his father, my great grandfather, whom he left in Eastern Europe.

Zeyda came to the United States and worked as a cantor (worship leader) and mohel (circumciser) in synagogues in various cities, finally settling in Washington, D.C. My father grew up in this Yiddish-speaking home in the poorer sections of Washington with the rest of the Jewish community. Dad graduated from high school in the middle of World War II, enlisted, and flew bombardier missions over Nazi Germany.

My mother and father wanted their children to have a better life than they had growing up. They worked hard. They gave us everything: a beautiful home, prosperous lifestyle, and a costly education. They wanted us to have more than they had. They invested themselves in us (God forgive us how we fail to appreciate the degree to which our parents dedicated their lives to bless us and provide for us). They paid tens of thousands of dollars to send me to an exclusive college.

I studied. I read. I searched through every possible field to uncover the meaning of life: philosophy, psychology, ancient literature, and Eastern religions. I sinned. I rebelled against my parents and every other form of authority. I became an atheist. But I could not get away from the deep inner yearning to know the real purpose of existence. My parents invested their lives to give me a platform to stand upon and to learn about life. I learned everything I could find to learn, and in my groping I stumbled upon the key to life: a revelation of the fact that God loves us, as expressed through the life of Jesus the Messiah. It is heart-breaking. It is glorious. Every person's life hangs in the balance between life and death. Every person, in one fashion or another, has a similar drama behind his or her life.

DRAWING YOU TO HIM

God has a plan for your life. He has one for me and He has one for you. From the time that we are born, God begins to call us toward that plan through the inner intuitive witness of our conscience (Romans 8:16). He draws us toward Him with invisible spiritual cords of love (Hosea 11:4).

Romans 8:30
Whom He predestined, these He also called.

From the moment you are born until the moment you are born again, God is calling you to Himself. It is not just that an individual is seeking for an answer. One Greater is attracting him invisibly with love. Different people around your life are bearing witness to you of God's love. People you do not know are praying for you. There is a conspiracy of love on your behalf.

I am always amazed at the seeming coincidences of people that God brings across our paths. Some time back, a college-age salesman knocked on our door with an inquiry. We asked him if he wanted to learn something about Yeshua, and he came in. It turned out that he was Jewish, that he went to the same high school as my wife, and that he was currently attending an Ivy League college similar to the one I went to. It was obvious that God had brought him to us. God was calling the young man to Himself. It was a divine appointment. We shared with him. He took a stack of books with an enthusiastic interest. What wonderful plans God must have for that young man. How God must love him! God was courting him and drawing him in love.

MAKING YOU RIGHTEOUS

God knew you before you were born. He had a plan for you when you were born. During your whole life after you were born, God has been calling you to Him. The next stage is to be justified. Justified is a word that means to be made righteous— to be made just.

Romans 8:30
Whom He called, these He also justified.

In the sight of God, we are made righteous in a moment. Yeshua exchanged His righteousness for our sin (II Corinthians 5:21). He became our substitute. He made atonement for us (Isaiah 53). In that moment of exchange, the human race was placed in right standing with God. That righteousness is applied to our lives the moment we receive it and apply it to ourselves. In that moment of radical change of character, you were made righteous.

You are not the same person you were before. You were unrighteous. Now you are justified. Now you are righteous. You were changed completely at the crossroads of faith. You were a sinner. Now you are not. You are in a new category in the eyes of God. You are in a different box. You are now a saint.

A saint is a justified believer in the process of being sanctified. You were a sinner. You believed in Yeshua. At the moment that you believed, you were defined as righteous or justified before God. Now you are in a new stage, in a new definition. This new stage is a process. It is a long process of becoming sanctified. A saint is a person in process of being sanctified. That's your new position. You are as different a person as if you had died, been buried, and then raised from the dead yourself. That is exactly what happens to you by faith in Messiah Jesus.

You are not to identify with the person you were previous to being born again. That is why Yeshua often changed people's names when they came to Him. You are to have a totally fresh, new, pure identity. It takes a long time to orient yourself to that new righteous identity. In fact, it takes a lifetime of realigning your thoughts and feelings to that new perspective (Romans 12:2; Ephesians 4:23). But the act of being justified before God only takes a moment.

MAKING YOU GLORIOUS

After a vessel is cleansed, it can be refilled. We not only have our inner spirit changed, but we receive God's own Spirit inside us. His Spirit is His glory. When we are filled with God's spirit, we are filled with His glory: we are glorified. "Glorified" means to be made glorious.

Romans 8:30
Whom He justified, these He also glorified.

Yeshua said that we would radiate light from our bodies and shine like the sun in the kingdom of our Father (Matthew 13:43). Moses shone with glory light from being in the presence of God (Exodus 34:29). Daniel said people would shine like the sun after the resurrection (Daniel 12:3). Yeshua shone with glory light at the Mount of the Transfiguration (Matthew 17:2).

In their battle song of victory, Deborah and Barak spoke of people shining like the sun (Judges 5:31).

God wants not just to erase what you have done wrong, but to give you something glorious to live for, both in the present time and in the hereafter. He has a destiny for you. He wants to give you a crown. He wants to make your life glorious. You can start living that life of glory right now. God wants to glorify you. The more that you can be glorified as His child, the more He gets glory out of it.

When you are justified, you become God's vessel. As you become glorified, you become a golden vessel. Paul told Timothy that anyone who chooses to cleanse himself of ungodly habits and low-level desires can become a glorious golden vessel (II Timothy 2:21). The purpose of the ministry of the New Covenant is to convey glory into the heart of the believer (II Corinthians 3:7-11). As we become more like Yeshua, that glorious nature is being transferred into us little by little (II Corinthians 3:18).

There are two stages to being made glorious. Stage A takes place during this lifetime while we have these mortal bodies. At this time the glory power is in our spirit, but limited by our clay bodies. (The Hebrew word for Adam or Man means "made out of clay.")

II Corinthians 4:7
But we have this treasure in earthen vessels, that the excellence of the power may be of God and not of us.

Stage B of the glorifying takes place after the resurrection when we receive revitalized bodies that are capable of handling unlimited glory power. Paul called that new kind of body a "glorified" body.

I Corinthians 15:42-43
**So also is the resurrection of the dead. The body . . .
is sown in dishonor, it is raised in glory. It is sown in
weakness, it is raised in power.**

How the body is glorified after the resurrection depends on
the degree we use it for holiness and righteousness before the
resurrection. It is what we do in this life that determines it. To
the degree that we suffer for our faith in this life, we will be
glorified in the world to come.

THE BUTTERFLY

God wants to make you into something glorious. This is the
pattern: God knew you before you were born. He had a plan
for you. He drew you to Himself. He completely transformed
you and recreated you into something righteous. Now He is
in the process of making you glorious. This process of being
made glorious is a drama in itself. You are like a caterpillar going
through the metamorphosis to emerge out of its cocoon as a
beautiful butterfly.

We all are being transformed into the same image from glory
to glory, just as by the Spirit of the Lord (II Corinthians 3:18).

NEGATIVE EVENTS

All the negative events that have happened to you in your life
highlight and contrast how special you are to God and how
much He loves you. The fact that the world hates you and
opposes you proves that you are of God and not of this world.
The world system hates God and it hates you. The more that
the world system hates you, the clearer it is that God loves you.
If the world hates God and hates you, then you must be loved
of God and not of the world. The fact that the world hates you

is proof that God has chosen you as His special treasure out of the world.

> ### John 15:18-19
> **If the world hates you, you know that it hated Me before it hated you. If you were of the world, the world would love its own. Yet because you are not of the world, but I chose you out of the world, therefore the world hates you.**

All the negative things that have happened to you because of your faith can be interpreted as a reverse indication that God has chosen you as precious to Him.

Why is this so important? As a pastor, I am aware of the stories behind many people's lives. Their lives have been filled with hurt, abuse, rejection, tragedy, and suffering. When I see the pain that people have gone through, my heart is broken. When God sees all the horrible things the world has done to you and how much the devil hates you, He is moved by compassion. His love goes out to you. It makes Him desire even more intensely, if that were possible, to protect you and prosper you.

Most people look at all the negative events of their lives and take these events as proof that they are no good and that God does not care about them. If you interpret the attacks of Satan as evidence of your own failure or the lack of God's love for you, you will be greatly hindered. Just as we are moved by special compassion to help a young child being picked on by neighborhood bullies, so does God have special love for you in the face of the devil's hatred of you. God sees your affliction and has sent His Word to deliver you. Sin opens the door for the devil to harm you. So do not sin, and do not let the painful events of your life make you feel condemned or worthless.

Indeed there is something heroic about the fact you made it through all those spiteful attacks of the enemy. Despite all the opposition of the combined forces of hell, you made it through to lay hold of eternal life. The more barriers stacked against you that you overcame highlight how much you love God. Yeshua still has scars on His resurrected body. Those scars are not proof of His failure and weakness, but of how much He was willing to go through for you. Do not let past failures get you down. Choose to see them as proof that nothing of evil can keep you away from loving God. Turn those past failures into testimonies of future victory (Romans 8:39). Use your past scars as a testimony of your tenacity to come to God and receive His love.

The Servant of the Lord is described as a root growing out of dry ground (Isaiah 53:2). Perhaps your life as well has been like a tender plant trying to grow up in the midst of hard concrete. The fact that there is all that harshness around you only makes it all the more precious that you love God. All the hardness of the concrete only highlights the tenderness of the plant and its determination to live. All the world has done against you only highlights how precious you are.

THE SOAP OPERA OF SOAP OPERAS

Why are people so fascinated with television serials? People are irresistibly drawn to know the story behind another person's life. Personal drama is compelling. Of course, with television one has only a poor substitute due to the low quality of most of the material presently offered. But there is a spiritual principle behind what makes people get so caught up in soap operas and serials. In reality every person's life is so extraordinarily interesting that there ought to be a book or movie about it.

I imagine the kingdom of God to start off with an extended testimonial banquet, where everyone's personal testimony will be shared, applauded, and appreciated. It will be the soap opera of soap operas, a grand "This is Your Life" show. Everyone will experience what you went through in your life. The people of God will surround you and cheer for you. Who knows? Maybe there will be a giant video screen with excerpts and special effects.

THE TRUTH ABOUT HISTORY

All that theater and drama are searching for; all that literature and biography are searching for; all that the arts and entertainment are searching for is to be found in the poignant drama behind every individual's life. In the unfolding of the testimonies of all the people of God throughout the ages will be found the glorious truth of what history was really all about. We will finally know what actually happened behind the events we read about in history books. The stories of the unsung heroes and heroines will be unveiled. The unheralded deeds of valor by those who gave their lives for faith and love will be brought to light. Every hidden and unknown act of unselfishness will be given its glorious reward in the presence of myriads of saints and angels.

All of mankind's creative talents are straining to arrive at an unknown something. Without God it is a vain thing. Instinctively man knows that every soul is precious. All artistic expression is an attempt to portray the inner values of the soul. Without God it is impossible. Your soul is precious to God. In the kingdom of God, we will be able to appreciate and enjoy the value of every person who walked by faith.

> *Hebrews 11:32-38*
> **And what more shall I say? For time would fail me to tell of Gideon and Barak and Samson and Jephthah, also of David and Samuel and the prophets: who through faith subdued kingdoms, worked righteousness, obtained promises, ...escaped the edge of the sword, out of weakness were made strong, became valiant in battle... Still others were stoned, they were sawn in two, were tempted, were slain with the sword. They wandered about... being destitute, afflicted, tormented – of whom the world was not worthy.**

We will enjoy all these testimonies together. Your life is one of them. You may look at your life and think that there is no great story to it. But that is not true. And your life can be exponentially more heroic if you will give yourself over to God in faith. Do not underestimate the importance of your own life. Do not miss the opportunity to make it count for God. We are all waiting to witness it.

THE UNVEILING OF GOD'S GLORY

How is God's glory to be revealed to mankind? How is it to be revealed to the angels, to the world, and to creation?

> **Romans 8:18**
> **For I consider that the sufferings of this present time are not worthy to be compared with the glory which shall be revealed in us.**

God's glory is to be revealed in us—through us. God does not primarily reveal His glory and His nature through a shining star, a snowflake, a rainbow, a humpback whale, a football game, a fast car, or a theological treatise. He reveals His glory through people who have given their lives to Him. God said that He revealed His glory through Messiah Jesus and that He would also reveal it through us (John 12:28; 17:1,22). You are the showplace of God's glory.

> **Romans 8:19**
> **The earnest expectation of the creation eagerly waits for the revealing of the sons of God.**

All of creation stands as an eternal audience watching the unveiling and manifestation of who you are. As you catch more revelation of who you are in Messiah, the more that revelation is revealed through you. As it is revealed into you, it is revealed out through you.

THE ANSWER TO ECOLOGY

The revealing of God's glory through you is what all of creation has been waiting for. All of God's creatures are waiting for you to catch a revelation of God's glory so that you in turn can reveal it to them. A tree or a dog or a polluted stream is not going to get a revelation of God's glory before you do.

Many young people mistakenly turned to ecology because they correctly perceived that nature was yearning for a liberating spiritual force (Romans 8:20-22). But nature is not the answer to our liberation; we are the answer to its liberation. The plants and the animals are not going to teach us about the glory of God; we are going to teach it to them. If we do not do it, they will just have to keep waiting.

All of creation has been eagerly waiting for you to catch a revelation of who you are in Messiah Jesus. As you gain your spiritual freedom, so in turn is the course of nature set free.

The grandest revelations of God yet to come are kept secret for us. Even the angels in heaven, and certainly the devils in hell, do not know what those revelations are. The secrets of God are communicated through His intimate Holy Spirit (I Corinthians 2:10-12). His Holy Spirit is in us. We are the first ones to get the news as it is released. We have a hot wire to God. The angels and the demons have to watch us and listen to what we say to find out what things God is revealing at the present moment.

Ephesians 3:10
...that now the manifold wisdom of God might be made known by the church to the principalities and powers in heavenly places...

Together with Yeshua, we are on center stage in the drama of the universe. The destiny of nature and history hangs in the balance as the people of God upon the earth struggle to grasp their own destiny in Messiah. As the plans of God are unfolded through you, so are they made manifest to all creation.

MOTIVATED FOR PURITY

God has given us these amazing promises: to be partakers of His eternal glory (John 17:22) and His divine nature (II Peter 1:4). In order to receive such great promises, we must have a pure heart. A teenager cannot be given keys to a car unless he first learns safe driving techniques and never to drive while under the influence of alcohol. A young woman with great physical beauty must learn to save that gift for her husband and to stay away from immorality. A wealthy person must learn how to use his finances without greed in integrity and generosity.

In the Israeli army part of basic training is "weapons purity." This is not referring to cleaning the rifle after use. It refers to the code of ethics that a weapon can only be used to protect the public under legitimate authority. A weapon can never be used for selfish or illegitimate reasons.

Throughout history God tried to bless people, but their character was weak and they used God's blessings for sinful purposes. Because our hearts are not ready, God has to withhold the blessings He desires to give us. Before Yeshua was given His anointed power to preach and heal, He had to pass three "character" tests at the hands of the devil (Luke 4, Matthew 4). Life in this world is a "moral test" from God to develop purity of heart. If we purge ourselves of pride, greed, anger, lust, unforgiveness and unfaithfulness, He can give us unlimited blessings.

II Timothy 2:21
...if anyone purifies himself of [these things], he will be a vessel meant for [glory].

Because of the great promises of glory, we have extra motivation to be pure and holy.

II Corinthians 7:1
Therefore, having these promises, beloved, let us cleanse ourselves from all filthiness of the flesh and spirit, perfecting holiness in the fear of God.

God punishes sin. Therefore we have the fear of God. The fear of God brings us into holiness so that we will not be punished.

Yet there is also a motivation by the positive promises of God. Not only will we not be punished if we stop sinning, but we will be ready to receive all the glorious blessing and destiny that God has planned for us.

We are also motivated to holiness by our love for others. We want to help them. If we lack holiness, we will disqualify ourselves as vessels of service to them. In order to have a sanctifying influence on others, we must first sanctify ourselves.

John 17:19
And for their sakes I sanctify Myself, so that they may also be sanctified by the truth.

Since holiness is God's character quality, we dedicate ourselves to be holy in order to be like Him. Without holiness we cannot come close to God, or even see Him.

Hebrews 12:14
Pursue... holiness, for without it no man will see the Lord.

Holiness is purity of heart; it is the ability to see God and to be like Him, it is moral perfection. Holiness is the quality of God that allows for all blessings, power and glory to come.

PERSONAL LIVES OF BIBLE CHARACTERS

As we read the stories of the people in the Bible, we should try to gain an insight into the drama behind their personal lives. Imagine, for example, God's seeing Abraham as a child still in Babylonia at Ur of the Chaldeans. God knew who Abraham was and who he was going to be. God moved him throughout different places in the Middle East, grooming Abraham's character through the various experiences.

Think of how God knew David as a little boy tending his sheep. David was the one that nobody noticed (perhaps you feel that nobody has noticed you). But God picked David out to be the king over Israel. God trained David in little things as David watched the sheep and protected them from the lion and the bear. In like manner, God sees you at times when no one else is noticing. He is training you in the little details of life to be of special service to Him.

Thinking of David as a little boy reminds me of how I enjoy seeing pictures of my wife as a little girl. God knew ahead of time that she was the perfect person to be my wife, and He was training her then in all the little things of life to be the wonderful person she is today. I am so grateful to God for doing that for me. I am so appreciative of the type of person my wife is. Long before we know what is going to happen, God is training us. Even when we are little children, God is preparing us for what is best for us.

The woman with the issue of blood who touched the hem of Yeshua's garment had a disease that made her a social pariah. She was disgusting in the eyes of her neighbors. She pressed through the brink of desperation to reach out to Yeshua. What love! What pathos! You will get to meet her one day. Her testimony can encourage you that whatever there is in your life that is like an issue of blood, whatever disgusting social disease you may seem to have, you are still precious and beloved to God.

Mary Magdalene was a demon-possessed woman. She was a despicable and unclean person. But Yeshua cleansed her. And of all the people who have ever lived throughout the history of man, she was the one chosen to be the first person that Yeshua appeared to when He was raised from the dead. Forever she will be the only person to bear that prestigious honor. What self-image problems she must have struggled with before that! How unworthy she must have seen herself! But God did not see her that way. God raises the lowly to high estate. However unworthy you may see yourself, God has plans to bestow special honor upon you. No matter how demonic and horrible you may have been, it is a joyous and easy thing for God to transform you. He's a "pro" at doing it.

THE PRODIGAL

The prodigal son lived the life of a pig. He squandered his life in the muck (Have you lived a period of your life as a pig? I did). All he could say to his father upon returning was, "Oh, I am so unworthy. I am not worthy to be called your son." But his father ran out to him. There was not a moment of hesitation or reluctance on the part of the father. The father sprang forward to meet him. No matter how you have wasted your life, God is running out to shower His love upon you. Despite your protests of unworthiness, God desires to bestow His finest upon you (Luke 15:20-22). Do not let the devil lie to you. God is running out to meet you with open arms. Whatever you have done wrong is not an issue if you will return to God. He loves you.

PETER'S TESTIMONY

Peter denied the Lord three times. The only thing Yeshua wanted to know about him was, "Do you love Me?" Forgiveness was not even an issue for Yeshua; it was a foregone conclusion. Are you struggling with guilt? Have you failed in your faithfulness to God? How do you think Peter felt? Judas betrayed Yeshua within a few hours of when Peter denied Him. Judas hanged himself. I have no doubt that the devil was screaming at Peter to do the same. Peter was fighting for his life to overcome thoughts of suicide. Perhaps one of the other disciples in a moment of ill temper said to Peter, "You're no better than Judas. Why do you not do the same?"

Have you ever been depressed? Have you struggled with feelings of hopelessness or suicide? Look what Yeshua said to Peter: "I do not care even that you denied Me. If you love Me, here, take my sheep" (John 21:15-17). I am still willing to trust you with everything I have." God is saying that to you as well. "Even if you have denied Me, if you will come back to Me in love, I will forgive you and trust you and restore to you everything I had in mind for you."

PAUL'S TESTIMONY

Before the apostle Paul was converted, he went around having believers killed and thrown in jail. The Bible says he breathed forth threats and violence (Acts 9:1). He was nasty and vengeful. He had done so much damage to the believers that at first no one would believe him that he had come to know the Lord.

Acts 9:26
When Saul had come to Jerusalem, he tried to join the disciples, but they were all afraid of him and did not believe that he was a disciple.

The other believers did not want to trust Paul or receive him. How painful that must have been! His friends were his enemies, and his enemies were his friends. First he had gone one way and then the next. Now he was pouring out his life for the kingdom of God, and his heart was breaking over the very suspicions that he had sown. Powerful forces were pressing Paul this way and that.

What a dramatic moment it must have been when it dawned upon the other disciples that this man was now their friend! What inner struggles must have been going on for all involved! But despite all this turmoil and psychological pressure against him, Paul emerged to be able to give his life to God as few men ever have.

BE OF GOOD CHEER

Whatever barriers you face, do not give up. Whatever the stress that comes against you, look to the Lord and He will see you through. God loves you. You are the apple of His eye and the target of His affection. God has a glorious plan for your life. You are special, unique and precious in His sight.

The stories of these men and women were not given to impress us. They were given to encourage us not to give up. Let us take courage then. Let us walk in faith even as they did. Life can be a wonderful adventure when we give ourselves into God's hands.

John 16:33
In the world you will have tribulation; but be of good cheer, I have overcome the world.

What encouraging words these are from the lips of Messiah Yeshua Himself! In Him we also have overcome the world (I John 5:4-5). In God's eyes we are more than conquerors (Romans 8:37). Through His strength there is nothing we cannot do

(Philippians 4:13). If God is for you, it does not matter if the rest of the world is against you (Romans 8:31).

Be of good cheer. Get out there and turn the world upside-down (Acts 17:6). It needs it.

APPENDIX
THE INNER MAN

I Peter 3:4 – . . . The hidden man of the heart.

Romans 7:22 – I delight in the law of God according to the inward man.

II Corinthians 4:16 – Even though the outward man is perishing, the inward man is being renewed day by day.

Ephesians 3:16 – . . . Be strengthened with might through His Spirit in the inner man.

Ephesians 4:23-24 – Be renewed in the spirit of your mind, and that you put on the new man which was created according to God, in righteousness and true holiness.

Ephesians 4:22 – Put off, concerning your former conduct, the old man which grows corrupt according to deceitful lusts.

I John 3:6,9 – Whoever abides in Him does not sin. Whoever sins has neither known Him nor seen Him. Whoever has been born of God does not sin, for His seed remains in him; and he cannot sin, because he has been born of God.

I John 4:17 – . . . As He is, so are we in this world.

II Corinthians 5:17 – If anyone is in Messiah, he is a new creation; old things have passed away; behold, all things have become new.

Galatians 6:15 – For in Messiah Yeshua neither circumcision nor uncircumcision avails anything, but a new creation.

II Corinthians 5:21 – ... That we might become the righteousness of God in Him.

Luke 1:35 – That holy thing that shall be born of you shall be called the Son of God.

Colossians 3:9-10 – . . . Since you have put off the old man with his deeds, and have put on the new man who is renewed in knowledge according to the image of Him who created Him.

Romans 7:20 – If I do what I will not to do, it is no longer I who do it, but sin that dwells in me.

II Corinthians 3:18 – But we all, as with unveiled face, beholding as in a mirror the glory of the Lord, are being transformed into the same image from glory to glory.

Romans 8:16-17 – The Spirit Himself bears witness with our spirit that we are children of God, and if children, then heirs— heirs of God and joint-heirs with Messiah.

James 2:26 – The body without the spirit is dead.

I John 5:4 – Whatever is born of God, overcomes the world.

Ephesians 2:10 – We are His workmanship, created in Messiah Yeshua for good works, which God prepared beforehand that we should walk in them.

Proverbs 23:7 – As he thinks in his heart, so is he.

John 17:16 – They are not of the world, just as I am not of the world.

I John 4:4 – He who is in you is greater than he who is in the world.

I John 3:2 – Now we are the children of God; and it has not yet been revealed what we shall be, but we know that when He is revealed, we shall be like Him, for we shall see Him as He is.

Philippians 4:13 – I can do all things through Messiah who strengthens me.

Romans 8:29 – That He [Yeshua] might be the firstborn among many brethren.

Hebrews 2:10-11 – In bringing many sons to glory . . . He [Yeshua] is not ashamed to call them brethren.

Romans 8:37 – Yet in all these things we are more than conquerors through Him who loved us.

II Peter 1:4 – That through these [promises] you may be partakers of the divine nature.

Asher Intrater, along with his wife Betty, is the senoir leader of Ahavat Yeshua congregation in Jerusalem, Tiferet Yeshua congregation in Tel Aviv, and the Revive Israel ministry team. Their work has included El Shaddai Congregation in Frederick, Maryland, Netivyah Ministries in Jerusalem with Joseph Shulam, the Messianic Jewish Alliance of Israel and preaching in congregations and conferences throughout Israel and the nations. Asher is also one of the founders of Tikkun Ministries International with Dan Juster and Eitan Shishkoff. He has degrees from Harvard University, Baltimore Hebrew College, and Messiah Biblical Institute and is the co-author with Dan Juster of *Israel, The Church and the Last Days*, the author of *Covenant Relationships, The Apple of His Eye, The Five Streams, From Iraq to Armageddon, What Does the Bible Really Say About the Land?, Who Ate Lunch with Abraham?* and numerous original witnessing tracts in Hebrew. Their current ministry priority is to raise up young Israeli believers into ministry through congregational life, daily prayer and praise watches, a discipleship training center, and personal evangelism to native Israelis. Revive Israel's email update is currently being translated weekly into 16 languages.

For more information, and to receive ministry updates, please visit **www.reviveisrael.org**